EDINBUR

Postcard Book

24 Classic Photographs by Col.

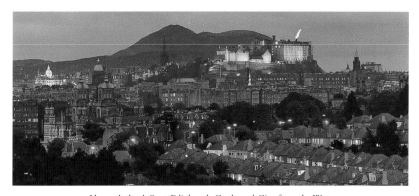

Above: Arthur's Seat, Edinburgh Castle and City from the West.
Front cover photograph: Edinburgh Castle and City from Salisbury Crags.
Back cover photograph: Edinburgh Castle, Princes Street and Princes Street Gardens.

LOMOND BOOKS
EDINBURGH • SCOTLAND

EDINBURGH

Built on seven hills, overlooking the sea and the Firth of Forth, Scotland's capital city enjoys a stunning position. Add in its medieval roots and graceful Georgian New Town, its museums, galleries and world-famous festival, and one can understand why Edinburgh is such a popular destination. The city often inspires a deep affection among its many visitors – a feeling shared by those who are fortunate enough to live here.

Since it was founded in the eleventh century, people's eyes have always been drawn to the city's cliff-top fortress that dominates the sky-line from all sides. For much of its history, Edinburgh was a walled hill-top town huddled round its castle for protection against the perennial threat of invasion. Much of the Old Town life revolved around a single street, which by the time of Mary Queen of Scots had become known as the Royal Mile, connecting the Castle with the Palace of Holyroodhouse.

Two hundred years ago, with the Old Town bursting at the seams, it was decided to build a New Town full of wide avenues, elegant crescents and imposing squares to the north. Since then Edinburgh has continued to grow northwards down to the sea-shore and risen to the south towards the Pentland Hills.

Long established as an international seat of learning and culture, with its thriving university, Edinburgh has evolved into a bustling, modern capital, complete with its long-awaited Parliament. Yet Edinburgh has retained its timeless heart and soul and remains for many, one of the most beautiful cities in Britain.

First published in Great Britain in 2001 by Lomond Books, 36 West Shore Road, Granton, Edinburgh EH5 1QD Reprinted 2003
Photographs Copyright © Colin Baxter 2001 Text Copyright © Colin Baxter Photography Ltd 2001 Text by Tom Bruce-Gardyne
All rights reserved. No part of this book may be reproduced, stored in a retrieval system or transmitted in any form or by any means
without the prior written permission of the publishers. A CIP catalogue record for this book is available from the British Library.
ISBN 1 84204 031 6   Printed in China

Edinburgh Military Tattoo.
Photograph © Colin Baxter.

LOMOND BOOKS

*E*DINBURGH

Palace of Holyroodhouse
from Salisbury Crags.
Photograph © Colin Baxter.

LOMOND BOOKS

EDINBURGH

Edinburgh Castle, Princes Street
and Princes Street Gardens.
Photograph © Colin Baxter.

EDINBURGH

West Bow, The Grassmarket
and George Heriot's School.
Photograph © Colin Baxter.

LOMOND BOOKS

E D I N B U R G H

The City from Salisbury Crags.
Photograph © Colin Baxter.

LOMOND BOOKS

E D I N B U R G H

Victoria Street and Victoria Terrace.

LOMOND BOOKS

EDINBURGH

The Forth Bridge at dawn.
Photograph © Colin Baxter.

LOMOND BOOKS

E D I N B U R G H

Edinburgh Castle and Old Town
at dusk.
Photograph © Colin Baxter.

LOMOND BOOKS

EDINBURGH

Deacon Brodie's Tavern,
The Royal Mile.
Photograph © Colin Baxter.

LOMOND BOOKS

EDINBURGH

Edinburgh Castle.
Photograph © Colin Baxter.

E DINBURGH

The Old Town and St Giles'
Cathedral.
Photograph © Colin Baxter.

LOMOND BOOKS

EDINBURGH

The City from Calton Hill.
Photograph © Colin Baxter.

LOMOND BOOKS

*E*DINBURGH

Edinburgh Castle and City
from Salisbury Crags.
Photograph © Colin Baxter.

LOMOND BOOKS

E D I N B U R G H

Old Town Rooftops and Calton Hill
from the Outlook Tower.
Photograph © Colin Baxter.

LOMOND BOOKS

*E*DINBURGH

Edinburgh Castle and
the Balmoral Hotel.
Photograph © Colin Baxter.

LOMOND BOOKS

E DINBURGH

New Town door.
Photograph © Colin Baxter.

LOMOND BOOKS

*E*DINBURGH

St Giles' Cathedral and
The Royal Mile.
Photograph © Colin Baxter.

EDINBURGH

Edinburgh Castle and
Ramsay Garden.
Photograph © Colin Baxter.

LOMOND BOOKS

EDINBURGH

Princes Street at dusk.
Photograph © Colin Baxter.

LOMOND BOOKS

E DINBURGH

Greyfriars Bobby.
Photograph © Colin Baxter.

E D I N B U R G H

The Scott Monument.
Photograph © Colin Baxter.

LOMOND BOOKS

E DINBURGH

Ramsay Garden.
Photograph © Colin Baxter.

LOMOND BOOKS

*E*DINBURGH

The Royal Mile and St Giles'
Cathedral.
Photograph © Colin Baxter.

LOMOND BOOKS

EDINBURGH

Edinburgh Castle and Bank
of Scotland at dusk.
Photograph © Colin Baxter.

EDINBURGH